A Call to Listen

Colleen Keating

A Call to Listen

Acknowledgements

Some of the poems in this book have won awards:
'daybreak over mt sondar', 1st place in Gum Blossom Poetry 2010;
'crimson rosella' and 'listen', Highly Commended
'morning lament', commended by judges in Poetica Christi Press
Poetry Competition 2011.

Some of the poems appeared previously in publications including
Eureka Street, The Mozzie, Poetrix, Poetry Matters, FreeXpresSion.
I am grateful to the editors for their dedication to poetry and
encouragement.

Some poems have also appeared in the following anthologies:
'maybe salacia' in Central Coast Poets Inc. Anthology, 2014;
'daybreak over mt sondar' and 'treading water' in *Our Women's Work*,
(Women Writers Network 2013);
'coastal walk', in *Poetrix Anthology* (Western Women Writers,
Issue 40, May 2013);
'morning lament' and 'renewal' in *Taking Flight*
(Poetica Christi Press, 2013).

I would like to thank convenor Siobhan Colman and members of the
Women Writers Network, and Norm Neill and fellow poets of the
Wednesday Night Poets, both at the NSW Writers Centre, Rozelle,
for their positive critique and affirmation.

Thank you to Margaret Hede and Michael Keating
for the final edit of my work.

Appreciation to Decima Wraxall for her friendship, and especially my
loving appreciation to Michael for his constant presence and patience.

A Call to Listen
ISBN 978 1 74027 896 6
Copyright © text Colleen Keating 2014
Cover photo by Elizabeth Keating-Jones,
taken at The Entrance, Central Coast, NSW, 2014

First published 2014
Reprinted 2016

GINNINDERRA PRESS
PO Box 3461 Port Adelaide SA 5015
www.ginninderrapress.com.au

Contents

We are but travellers here	9
dawn	11
darginyung	12
daybreak over mt sondar	13
milky way dreaming	14
we are but travellers here	15
ormiston pound	16
coolamon dreaming	17
abandoned	19
vicissitudes of lake eyre	20
parachilna rumble	21
The web	23
almost dawn	25
anticipation	26
the web	27
early morning rain	28
from my bedroom window	29
sisters	30
rendezvous	31
she is flower enough	32
at a takoyaki bar	33
rainy day woman	35
my son	36
my grandson	37
in the clouds	38
Treading water	41
treading water	43
dawn	44
maybe salacia	45

coastal walk	46
return of persephone	47
lying on the beach	48
coxcombry	49
caprice	50
catching time	51
solitaire	52
southerly buster	53
the wharf	55
turning the tide	56
The smell of parsley	**57**
listen	59
winter morning walk	60
soul's winter	61
zen moment	62
renaissance	63
saving the jacaranda	65
solitary tomato plant	66
the smell of parsley	68
moments in our garden	69
The shadow we chase	**71**
guantanamo bay	73
terrorism	74
war on terror	75
Between the wings of the crow	**77**
morning lament	79
street madonna	80
desert gaol	82
requiem for a suicide bomber	83
leased war	85

this poem is about silence	86
lights a candle	88

A call to listen — 89

the space between	91
hypnotised	92
shattered	93
anzac	94
escaping with cezanne	95
august mornings in hiroshima	96
at the nursing home	99
how to love a rock	100
going going	101
hiroshima sixty-five years on	102
fromelles 2009	103
chance encounter	104
dispossession	105
dispossession 2	106
dispossession 3	108
tokyo markets	109
soka-eki	111
tokyo train	112

Cockatoo clamour — 113

upon waking	115
the black-shouldered hawk	116
crimson rosella	117
aerodynamics of a feather	118
a black swan event	119
baptism by fire	121
learning to take time	122
wild no longer	123

We are but travellers here

dawn

for michael

before i open my eyes
in the morning
i feel your presence
and know the day
has begun beautifully

darginyung

welcome to country   drones
        the didgeridoo   its spirit
                circles the hollowed wood

sings the darkness into dawn
        and in its dancing rhythm
                the dreaming drifts in

daybreak over mt sondar

in the beginning
air static as a nylon petticoat pulled over my hair
fingerprints of ruby red
betray the world dark coloured
the arc of dawn flexes
stirs mt sondar
an awakening blush
flutters fire red catching
namatjira's mountain
blood red

as i sit here   it pulsates
the sun   not yet over the horizon
like an intruder rushes in
steals every shade and shadow

this mountain lies in the country with poise
immortalised in a gown of purple and blue
like a sleeping goddess behind glass

yet the rattle of chains and padlock
thump like a heartbeat against my ribs
as in the nearby town
for a dollar
kids still buy a rusty jam tin of petrol

milky way dreaming

sun ablaze
dark skin
shines with sweat
her eyes look up   catch me

she sits on the earth
a red sandy space
at the edge of the alice springs mall
her canvas held down
by four small rocks

milky way dreaming

a sash of silver gossamer
arches across the black canvas
in a brilliance of stars
to the side seven dotted circles
she points
names the seven sisters

only desert eyes know this sky
paint this song of stars
didgeridoo dancing stars
brimming
fiery-white and deep

now on my wall
framed

we are but travellers here

in desert country
outside alice springs
richly red rock rusted fiery
bruised and brush-worked to indigo
shimmers through hot air

a track like an ancient song line
marks a way
frisks intruders

needle spinifex claw
roots of river-gums
bulbous siphons   plunge defiantly
deep into dry river beds

we trudge heavily
sand shifts unevenly

bones picked clean
washed up   caught against tree trunks
from the last big wet
a warning this land is merciless
nemesis
teacher

at the end of each day
a truck delivers swags
food water
reminding us
we are but travellers here*

* we are but travellers here – Mary Mackillop

ormiston pound

we climb an ancient path
to the rattle of our tin mugs
and the chinkle of boots disturbing stones
as they shift awkwardly underfoot

quartzite
flanks each side
and summons up rough sharp spurs

serrated edges
like bread knives
cutting the sky
give direction

flints of mica catch the light
blinding and brooding black rocks watch
as menacing phantoms

at the top
we sit breathless
and hot
the wide expanse of ormiston pound
like an enormous bunker
lies below

air drifts with heat and layers of cool
we sit and listen to white man's story

while an acacia bush nearby
growing from a rocky outcrop
sings to me another story
on the dreaming wind

coolamon dreaming

desert night
a thousand stars drip
over our finke river camp in ormiston pound
dwarfed by walls of rock

heat sighs as it cools
gentle on our cheeks

now firelight flickers on our faces

smug in geological knowledge
that we are camped in a meteor crater
we lounge back
and listen
to the elder
weave her dreamtime stories
into the tapestry of creation
her eyes dark as night
draw us in

the baby star fell
our ancestors tell of a fierce light
its crash to this place

she points up

see the coolamon from where it fell
her finger curves the outline
of a black space in the sky

and still each day
its parents   the morning and evening star
circle the earth in search
of their fallen child

i sleep the dreaming
breathe the ancient air
in awe   feel connected
aware of the stars as my ancestors

i wake
to hues of mustard and ochre red
last curdles of smoke from the ashen fire
and watch the morning star
journey in cobalt-blue sky

coolamon – a basin-shaped wooden carry-dish made and used by some first peoples

abandoned

a fallen water tank
rusted blood red
rippled
as the sere ribs of a dead beast
lies half buried
in the shifting ochre red earth
against stony ruins
dominantly built

a witness
to the firefly hope
and belief
abandoned

to conquer nature

in south australia there are many ruins, remains from the hopeful who
built unaware of the goyder line that would be declared in 1865

vicissitudes of lake eyre

bleached salt pans
glint in a hostile sun
their mirage
a phantom deathtrap
in a land of unreachable horizons

yet sometimes flood waters
flow
crack the parched earth
eddy into the cavernous silence
and like touch arouses longing
water stirs
awakens a dormant world
into golumptuous life

fish like transparent slivers of glass
brine shrimp   trilling tadpoles
become a teaming ocean
luring flocks of birds to roost and feed

a million water birds in a desert sky
a paradise
till drought
kali with a flaming sword
banishes life once again

parachilna rumble

dangerous to blink
driving into parachilna
population seven
not even the dusty brown dog
gets up to greet us

the furrowed road
edged with dusty tuffs of salt bush
stretches to the horizon
in this boundless land

parachilna is a welcome stop

a hot hazy town
a red earth town
it glows a red clay aura
burnished red and dusty
even the old pepper trees
are dusty

the prarie pub
is famous for its FMG
Feral Mixed Grill
an antipasto of camel emu goat and kangaroo
quandongs natural limes and bush tomatoes
yet the sparkle of chilled white wine
makes the stop worth while

the barmen   like a town crier
calls
train on
and the pub quickly empties
to regroup
across the wide wide dusty street

a distant hum intrudes

chardonnay in hand
we watch the freight train
heavy with coal
ponderously lumber
like a gentle swarthy beast
towards us

the parachilna rumble begins
a heavy slow rumble
all three kilometres of it
with muffled grumbles
and slow clanks
hypnotic music of the outback

like children we practise counting
this head to tail migration
two hundred and twenty cars
it recedes in its own time
as the desert reclaims its silence

parachilna was once a town now a pub in south australia between
port augusta and leigh creek and west of the flinders ranges

The web

almost dawn

he turns
arms cocoon me
in an aura of warmth
his breath tingles
in the dip of my neck

my hand plays
reaches the wells of his desire
i hear him sigh

his hand moves over me
with the confidence of a cellist

vibrating
we lie together
curled
in the almost dawn

anticipation

thought of meeting you
gives ripples of warmth
skips my heart
steps too
the hum   the buzz
enough to lift off
with a scurry of anticipation
my mind sings
what delight to scan the crowd
like a thousand nodding daffodils
find your familiar smile
hurry closer
till eyes capture each the light
closer
reach trembling   touch
hold a beating heart lightly
as words unspoken
drift to the mind's quiet place

the web

curves and lines orbit
between the slate blue plumbago and the white azalea
illusive in the stare of the day   it spins out
jewelled glistening dew
long dried as noon had come

a butterfly   in flights of fantasy
each interlude on its terms
flits and flirts with a shimmer and quest
communing with the nectar of life

its next encounter   a delicious tangled seduction
contortionist struggle into the stillness of surrender
the yellow-ribboned spider winding with nimble fingers
caressing touch   a consummation

early morning rain

mouth wide open
tongue thrust out
to jab the flat metallic sky
jolt it into action
eyes tightly closed to taste
the full sensation of the rain
kerplopping on my tongue

fresh manna from heaven
its tickles   make me laugh
showers down my throat
into the marrow of my bones
arms high with cries from my heart
more please   more
it falls   pelts against my body
i jump in delight   splash
down into puddles

the sky crying
cleanses   makes new my body
wracked with sobs and bitter salty tears
wept through the night.

from my bedroom window

a low aching sky
colour of wet elephant skin
swathes its heavy hide around me
tunic for a warrior woman

blue flowering plumbago
laden with rain droplets
quivers in the breeze

a rainbow lorikeet dangles
from a drooping grevillea

the yellow-ribboned spider
orbited in diamond splendour
awaits her prey

the rusting gutter weeps a spangle of tears
ripples rhythmically the puddle it makes
its slow-tapping beat
becomes the music of this silver-slated day

sisters

we lunch together
in a cosy organic café
roast pumpkin soup with crusty bread
turmeric and ground peppercorns

share familiar laughter
love of being together

we celebrate
the milestone of another decade
and that word 'remission'
a green shoot springing
from the scarred black earth

we drink melon and apple juice
for their vitamins and minerals

and splurge
with our lust for life
on home-made lemon and lime tart
with fresh whipped cream
topped with a slice of lime

toast with a glass of bubbly
joie de vivre

rendezvous

she plumply blooms
flowery blouse
curved simple skirt
bobby-pinned hair
round smiling face

she sweeps the cobbled stones
around the entrance
to her shop on *calle de zaragoza*
tourist route to madrid's *plaza mayor*

she moves to a rhythm
her sweepings   her friendship offering

glances down the narrow way
then waves and blushes

the street cleaner in his eco-truck
moves towards her
nods
eases around her   about her
his wet angled spinning brooms roar
he smiles and continues on

glowingly she looks after him
content with her rendezvous

she is flower enough

loose hair caresses her shoulders
its pink streaks fall over her face
a shy flick
reveals a golden gypsy earring
and eyes that spark new bloom
the freshness of dawn

i reach out my hand
to touch the black velvet
in the folds of her red roses
and look up into her smile
catch her gaze

like pushing pause on a remote
the noise and haste of the flower markets
its busy orbit of colour and perfume
acrobatic swing of boxes and buckets
of tulips carnations and lilies
the pirouette of forklifts
the bustle
the call of bargains and buys
become still and mute

life rushes back
a trance broken with my whisper
three bunches of red roses please

at a takoyaki bar

by her smile in a sea of faces
on a busy street in Tokyo
we find each other

she elegant   petite   japanese
i australian in jeans jacket and backpack
her daughter our connection

at a *takoyaki* bar
we two women   two languages
tell the stories of our lives
deep mesmeric wells of story
as one can only do with a stranger
with the distance for perspective
noticing the far can be near

with banter of nods and laughter
we chat and listen
listen
with hearts and eyes

and with common feminine symbols
we understand each other

our sharing a shuttle
pulling weft across warp
no beginning no end
our fabric of conversation
seamless
and silence part of the weave

we enjoy the aroma of *takoyaki*
as it is prepared and cooked
share the meal
and together sip green tea

takoyaki is a sea food dish, a japanese speciality cooked and served
with ritual at the table sprinkled with bonito flakes and *aonori*

rainy day woman

oil paint drizzles
down a canvas
raining over
brushed collaged skin
alabaster
nuanced buff pink

a softly curving body
lies naked across a bed
open
a sacred text

orange cushions
luxuriate around her

chin rests on bent arm
fingers pensively
touch a lower lip

eyes
lowered
hold her mystery

my son

please don't go like this
there is another way
a word   a kiss
a nod

don't go like this
there's nothing i won't do

to go like this
in your pain and mine
is not the way

even in the anger
there is another way

however betrayed you feel
heart cries for us
please don't go like this

walls do not set us free

my grandson

gathered up
in my arms
warm and snuggled
is my grandson

he reaches out to explore
my nose
grasps my glasses
my earrings fascinate

his eyes shine with curiosity
smile with delight
his laughter is bountiful
his warm body melts me

i tell him it is a beautiful world
and it is

yet in the background
i know it too is a troubled world

my eyes mirror a world of love
and i hold him ever closer

in the clouds

as a child i loved to lie on grass
see shapes in clouds
i still see feathers and angels

as a poet i have dreamt of clouds
marshmallow at sunset
cauliflower by day
ruffled at dusk

on my new mac air
i compose a first draft
push save
and it goes to icloud

then the panic sets in
i rush outside
except for a tiny airbrush
cloudless

should have done this yesterday
when there was a swarm of clouds
yet there was fog then
surely that's not ideal

this would only be reliable
if we lived under a cloud
far too gloomy for me

some say i have my head in the clouds
maybe
i would like to live on cloud nine
but that's not good for a writer

sometimes on the horizon
i see a cloud-bank
but no one trusts banks today
i know we have cloudbursts especially in summer
what will happen to my poem then

maybe icloud beclouds the issue

cumulus although poetic are unstable
glinting cirrus are too high and made of crystal
nimbus would serve the purpose thick and grey
but stratus are soft and luxurious
my poem would swoon curled up there

Treading water

treading water

there is a touch of the transcendent
on the horizon today   the sky spreads
like the sound of a symphony   and shadows
the deep slate of sea with its surge
of rolling energy   tufts of crested foam
and sweeps of spindrift thrown in the air like hands of praise

out there crouches a small grey boat
bobbing in and out of view
a sea snail with its feelers poised

maybe fishermen or divers near a hidden reef
maybe sailors to catch the coloured winds of the dawn
i do not expect to know more

ebb tide   the hollowed waves
like hungry mouths gulp
stretch languidly to the edge
lull like the pause between briny breaths
then recede

on the shoreline of my mind
thoughts tread water
more lonely than the boat on the slate-grey sea
as my footprints meld with the tide

back home i continue
to stream a shelf of diaries

dawn

her night gown falls
she opens for the majesty
of morning
her young maiden blush
fills the sky

the ocean
delights
with a shimmering smile

on the headland
a poet
like her lover
gazes in awe
ponders her beauty
and grapples for words

maybe salacia

she walks the beach
        scanning shells on the edge
in a loosely tied sarong
        hair swept up under a wide brim hat
        face lined with many lifetimes

fishermen and sailors nod and smile
sea gulls rummaging along the shore hardly notice

she walks barefoot on the sea-soaked sand
        tracing the waving wrinkled water mark
        bites of the briny sea at her toes

        she bends to receive tumbled gifts
        golden whelks   nippled periwinkles
        spindled limpets   black nerites   spotted voluted
cowries

some say she listens to the music of the sea
        others say she's a drifter
        or perhaps
        an artist living her art
        a poet living a poem
some say she belongs to the deep
maybe goddess of the sea

now and then she gazes out
        to where the sea and sky converge
        as if she yearns
        to slip between the sentinels of crashing waves
to her home beyond

coastal walk

my eyes trace lines
that curve and swirl
track contours and circled altars
waiting their tide reunion
where only soft padded periwinkles
and sharp edged oyster shells venture
landscapes of sculptures composed
by the dreamtime of water wind and sand
a patterned mosaic
dioramas unfolding
like silken threads from a mulberry leaf

each line   each ripple
a stretch mark   wrinkle   scar
has its story

with the tide the ocean
rolls and thunders
sometimes her fingers
like talons scratch and claw
yet eternally patient
her hands caress
love and mould
soothe the hardened bones and sinews
smooth and soften the violent edges
touch the secret caverns
and with each tide seduce a little more

return of persephone

on a night-blue sea
still as lovers wrapped in slumber
persephone returns

the world is touched
handmaiden clouds stir

blush   pulsate gold
at the edge of anticipation

the sea catches the moment
shimmers like ruffled satin

orange sand-dune clouds high above
hang on the moment

two in a canoe glide smoothly
dark and small on the ocean

an outboard putters
towards fishing grounds

flocks of gulls flash past
wings light up in their sweep

galahs flirt
magpies motif the dawn

flush of technicolour   fires
dancing pomegranate-red
into a moment of ecstasy

lying on the beach

in leafy-pandanus shade
a floppy summer hat
covers my face

through its plaited fibres
sky shimmers   purple blue   red and gold

ocean unaware of its charm
stretches languidly towards me
with a lullaby
my breath eavesdrops on its rhythm
warm sand pillows me
sifts between my fingers
curls between my toes

and i stay all morning
one with sand and sea and sky
being all this
it being all me

coxcombry

wind whips up a moody day
buffs a motley sky

rain squalls in   tide
busts out with fullness
slaps the rocks in glib elation

a wildness of waves
dizzily flamboyant
with flustered curl and spin
jostle their way to shore
plumed dandies together in a parade

rugged-up surfers
lean against their vans
scan the ocean   boards still on their racks
envious of these coxcomb waves

caprice

yesterday
an unflinching southerly
whipped up a frenzy
the outer rocks of the *bombora*
pointed and sharp
screamed in fury
a foaming dark monster
pounded   roared   devoured
all in its wake

today
a silken cloak
masks the *bombora*
liquid silver waves scroll past
sapphire-tipped
fan gently onto the sand
with a whisper

on the edge
gazing to where sea and sky are one
my curled toes squelch wet sand

extravagance excites
moods disturb
mystery seduces

catching time

its not so easy now
to walk on sand
my sister and i amble
aware of the strength of the breeze
that it might be a little easier walking back
aware of the challenging tilt
caught already by a wave
unable to get out of its way in time

we reminisce
how we ran and frolicked in the surf
how we chased each other
caught and plunged sand
down each others bathers
and laugh at our once-upon-a-time playfulness

we stop
catch our breath

on the grassy bank
a heron   grey and sleek
with devouring eyes
stalks stealthily
its long neck
rippling
like dune grass in the breeze
and peewees
giggling maids-in-waiting
follow behind

just for now
time stands still

solitaire

a dormitory of cormorants sleep
strung out like dracula's washing
on phosphate denuded branches
of norfolk pines
high above rippled
navy water of tuggerah lake

far to the west the watigan range
stills
the last plum flush of the day

the night sky
dimly at first
breathes thousands of tiny lights

walking alone
along the jetty

i hear a stir
shiver of reeds
vagrant swish of water

and glimpse
a cormorant

i stand and watch it
dive resurface dive again

in darkest water
playing alone

southerly buster

on a pearly-silver day
a celestial backdrop
of slanted shafts of light
cloud-ripe
for a bearded god
to peer over
with smile or frown

i rambled
around reefy outcrops
perfect for crashing spindrift displays
with miniature ocean-worlds at my feet

but the weather turned

swirling charcoal wind
like cold grey dragon's breath
heaved
scudded sand
whipped my legs making
my walk a huddled hurry
scurrying to beat the squall.

a banksia near the sand
saved the soaking that could have been
honey dew cones
dripped
as i crouched for shelter

my walk cut short
the sea shrouded
vista gone
i could've felt alone
but two birds joined me
masked lapwing plovers
their long-legs danced
delighting this turn around day

the wharf

is safe to stand on
or dive deeply off

into the wet
give my body
my whole face in

after the first stir
ripples of warmth
would spread like waves
bliss with the touch
and taste   a new landscape
infinite possibilities of treasure
no feel for oysters sharp on rocks

the blue-green summers' ocean
murmurs   come   play
my toes curl   fumble
on the grey weather-dried edge

turning the tide

it's a big sky   the horizon
where the sea meets it
would be a lonely line
except for the old man who keeps it company

he knows the weathers personally
sits   watches over the lake's journey into the sea
keeps the tides on track
shepherds their turning   checks they're on time

what do you do when it's all done
leathery face   salty beard
his blood-shot eyes
smile contentedly

The smell of parsley

listen

bowed trees sleep
tresses crunch at their feet
hound of wind moans
rhyme with rustle tones
come closer
listen
snick on grass
wake of bird
seed on wing
leaf brush on air
crack and rustle of skink
in their leaf litter rush of hide-and-seek
cricket-croaks
fruitfly-drone
frog-plonk in pond
snap of seed-pod
kerplop of fruit and berry
and in the underworld
rub of beetle and ant
the only other sound
easy drift
of vesper leaves
settling
to a hush
this seasonal paradigm
whispers its arrival
no fuss
except it's time

winter morning walk

come with me
feel the shrill bell-tingle
of the morning on your face
leave your ears bare to listen

unfurl yourself
like the pocket magnolia bud
peeping from its birthing cocoon
its curiosity insatiable
knowing it is glorious

distinguish whips and chortles and chirps
and screech of the sulphur-crested cockatoo
high above in the blue gum

smile at the showy red camellia
its carpet of colour reflecting its flamboyance
take in that orange blossom scent

kneel before the snow bells
profuse like lilies of the field
below the wisteria's bare brambles

rub hands
with the pepper tree foliage
let its aroma play in your mind

ah what joy
is this winter morning walk
around the block

soul's winter

on the birth of my grandson

waiting in winter
on the cusp of spring
for a baby to be born
feels as if the world
has taken a vow of silence
and time is paralysed

it amazes me how close is death
to the birth of new life

outside a straggly wet mop of a day
droops in
skeletal limbs of trees x-rayed against sky
shudder like brittle bones
breathing   just a little
tremulously

their cold black presence
chills my blood
stirs thoughts of death
i sense its shadow
shiver in its grip

my heart fumbles
like one lost in a dark night
stunned in the impasse of unknowing

i want to believe that this will change
and that I will soon
be dazzled

and i am

zen moment

a tawny leaf

clothed
nourished
the tree

lived its time
served its purpose

takes its leave
surrenders

falls

how gently it falls
falling
falling
its fluttered spin
air-cushioned down

received
lightly
silently
by the earth

renaissance

it was a long dry
the underbelly of the dam
in the far paddock
exposed tyres   a rusted trap   machinery
old wheels and discarded petrol drums

after the rains
sounds from the dam call
through the scrub
i follow the once hard dusty track
now a squelch of mustard clay
and sticky wet paspalum knee deep

dank-scented saplings and surviving gums
cocoon new life
saffron-blue water lilies
crowd the iron-black water
needles of wind cross stitch the surface
falling seed pods dip of willow
the scud of iridescent ducks
zip of stippled dragon wings
and dart-tilt-skim of arrowed swallows
overlay the pattern

at the far end
half-hidden in the reeds
lies a rotting mossy log
a diving board from my childhood days

crickets   frogs   birds in chorus
and gregarious squeals
from two busy masked lapwings
on the bank
create a bush symphony

here is my place of refuge
it feels like a coming home
the roots of an old gum extend
comfortable arms
i sit in their embrace
listen
and watch

an egret stalk its prey

saving the jacaranda

the line for the new concrete
drainage pipe
runs under the massive old jacaranda

meticulous to protect its roots
day after day the council men
ratty and mole in fluorescent yellow
dig a man-made warren
wide and deep

exposed roots
stretch and coil like bearded monsters
from a tenebrous underworld
smelling earthy airless damp

then overseen by an arborist
a crane lowers the pipe into place
and this private world is reclaimed

a year on
standing before its gnarled trunk
on a lilac path
i am corralled in its aura
of blossom-laden branches
and i rejoice with the breeze
in whispered mantras

solitary tomato plant

feast your eyes on the green
                             a healing colour
said hildegard of bingen
let its thousand shades and dappled ways
imbue your eyes
give resilience

i carry her words into my garden
plant out chilli   chives and coriander
zucchini   lettuce of different kin and basil

and a solitary weedy tomato plant from the throw-out table
there's a pact between us
not just to survive
we will thrive

i prepare the soil with extra blood-and-bone
                     gently plant it out   settle it in
with stakes for it to climb
                     circle with sawdust to ward off those
                                that love to munch
under the sprinkler
limp leaves uncurl
sit up so vibrantly
i hear it grow

in the garden i come alive
the soil
with its rich textured compost
feels good
i marvel
                        my scraps   now this wonder
the worms
have worked their magic

a kookaburra sits above
a magpie stalks
                            turned soil their turn on

smell of sun-warmed grass
lightly   so lightly wafts
i stand   stretch   watch a white butterfly hover

in shorts and sleeveless top
i enjoy the sun
resilient in my gardening boots and gloves
i manoeuvre the wheelbarrow
and we patiently wait to bloom

the smell of parsley

tend the garden
after the rains
knee deep
in wet grass
up to your elbows in soil
and worms
and snails
and niff of compost

marvel at the ramble
of a pumpkin vine
a stray seed gone free

linger in the fragrance
of chives and basil
coriander   rocket   and mint
and the smell of parsley

what is the smell of parsley?

savour their bouquet
be jubilant
with the flirt of white moths
and the canticle on the branch above
dwell on your knees
as if in prayer
tending the garden

moments in our garden

camellia

with bright red flowers
like pinned on brooches
decorating a drag-queen's gown
the camellia
flamboyantly
brightens the low winter sky

waiting

magnolia branches
stark in a moody sky
their bristly twigs
dressed barely
in tight furry buds
waiting to capitulate

star magnolia

one capricious bud
peeps
from its furry coat
too curious to await
the season
for its unfolding

the blue gum

the sagacious eucalypt
sheds sienna-singed
motley
smile-shaped leaves
yet still shares
its dappled shade

a return

ah what joy
chortle of the magpies
and their foray into the garden
means they have returned to nest
and i am still here
to welcome their offspring

The shadow we chase

guantanamo bay

this is a poem not to be read aloud
for it speaks of solitary confinement
torture and words like water boarding
it speaks of men
now aliens on this planet
with nowhere to call home
and no legal system
to try them

these men
have shackles
wear orange overalls
live in barbed wire cages

offshore

this is all we know
we don't hear their cries
we don't even know names

terrorism

underbelly
with sleek scales
tranced by the light
being victim
breeds revenge
spawning
powerless consent

like snakes pinioned
in rage
lash out
begetting rage
ouroboros-like
spiralling down
eyes dim in the dark

terrorism
is one's power
and one's fear

war on terror

its coming
through a hole in the air

we breathe its fiery breath
hear its dark-beating heart
coming at you and you
stalks every hourly news

terror is real
ask one blinded
by the black spot of fear

but it's not there

you can't bomb the intangible
drones can't destroy terror
yet can a war on terror be an act of terror

all we have is a voice
to say resist
violence does not work

if the shadow we chase
is caught
it will be our own

Between the wings of the crow

morning lament

the morning begins with the crow
its articulated screech
takes me back to my fourth-grade teacher
and world of long division
incomprehensible

the digital radio lights up
the dark of night is past
secret fears
scuttling crabs of the heart
dart into hiding

morning news like canned laughter
mocks me
as leaders in a world of illusion
seize loop holes
to button me down with their spin

between the wings of the crow
is stored anguish
and mourning   women's lament
under dark skies lit by destructive fire

dawn becomes glare
stares me down
blindingly

and the crow mocks
as it flies away
beyond consciousness

street madonna

she was there yesterday
quiet as a fresco
sunlit olive skin   eyes lowered
a shawl and joyful skirt

i felt a jolt
passed quickly by

> walk picasso's footsteps
> barcelona's gothic quarter
> marvel at ancient roman walls
> sip coffee in the bohemian-quarter *kats*
> inhale the vibe of past artists writers poets

she is there again today
on the cold stone steps
near the ornately carved doors
her presence loud

i was warned
walk on
but a voice inside says
this is different

in the cathedral the rose window
plays its colours
mother and baby statue
glows in candle light

on my way out
a fumble in my heart
makes me halt
i scan her face

she looks up   eyes hook me
draw me   she smiles
the cup in her hand
rattles

under her mantle
a baby cradled in her lap
reaches out

desert gaol

i'm haunted by a photo scene
a makeshift desert gaol
with barbed wire as a barricade
men with bare feet
wearing simple garb white *djellaba*
hands tied behind their backs
over their heads plain black sacks
crowded and cowering they sit

near one a tiny child leans
toes digging into the sand
the man unable to reach out a hand
to comfort or reassure

often in my dreams
i wonder what became of them

requiem for a suicide bomber

twice each day
she passes through the check point
the eye of a needle
portal of a war-torn heart
to work   on the other side
the concrete wall cuts
a vandal's knife
through her uncle's farm

on this day
shuffling through   eyes lowered
she shows her work pass

well polished black boots
feet planted squarely apart
block her way

she looks up
his eyes
malevolent   intent
blinding as the light off the barrel of his gun
her fear
his turn on

he taunts
pulls her hard against his uniformed body
like an inflatable sex doll
laughs at her impotent disgust
and his power

a year later
with posture of defeat
a heavy belt around her waist
steadfast
she walks into a busy marketplace
her body
her weapon

leased war

in the photo
a child stares
into a blood-splattered car

in his heart
what seeds are planted

what tangles and grows
in a harsh elegiac landscape
of desert sand and rubble

two women dead   the news said
shot by hired security guards
answerable to none
they get the job done
with privatised weapons
privatised tanks   ammunition

no more mention of the child
growing up in his homeland
a privatised crucible of war

this poem is about silence

words get in the way of silence
it needs a blank page
it needs space
in silence there can be longing
there can be anticipation
hostile   intimate
you can hear it
in the pin-drop moment between bow and string

you can feel it between breaths

the inarticulate use of violence for expression
is this silence?

can you say the sharp sickle moon
that glows on a dark winter sky is silent?

when one turns their back in silence
silence is palpable
and what of a silence imposed in fear

silence can be loud

a silent protest
even without poster or placard is loud

when the powerless stitch their lips together
with needle and fishing line
is this silence
even if tears still fall

evil thrives under silence

a poem about silence
needs to be loud
to be heard

lights a candle

and it comes to pass
we misplace our hearts
lose the song
forget the dance
break our tambourines
turn our backs
tremble with fear

when the unknown arrives
close doors

no names
no stories
no refugees
only a coined word
illegals

alleviates responsibility
croons amnesia

and in time
forget our humanity

unless someone like us…

A call to listen

the space between

two women poets
hang side by side
in the portrait gallery

               contained now

the space between
has its story
of times around the kitchen table
when these two women
saw other ways of being

words their weapon
justice   their spirited charge
to break the wall of apathy
lift us beyond its rubble
give us new possibilities

oodgeroo noonuccal   whitewashed as kath walker
with sombre dark eyes and black skin

she anchored herself in hope
       survived its instability
and kept it alive

judith wright   social conscience
soft wrinkled sun-dried face in wide brimmed hat

a peace warrior she raged at injustice
her words   a cry
against ignorance and greed
together they gaze out
       calling us to listen

oodgeroo noonuccal (1920–1993), judith wright (1915–2000) –
poets, activists and friends

hypnotised

on victoria island near vancouver

the sun could be canonised as a miracle worker
it hangs mildly in the sky
long and lingering
here on the forty-ninth parallel

its holy hands
turn this sullen inland sea to shimmering silver
if it were a shining mirror
one could say the sea sees itself
and shyly smiles

like the water's thoughts
tiny fish rise   ripple the surface
and quieten again

i stay quiet
allow the useless constant nibbles of my thoughts
to settle into the deep

shattered

crisis of faith

1

in the morning light   a thousand prisms
reveal colours never seen
a comet strikes the day
shattered glass barrier broken
exposed and vulnerable
empty space leaves nowhere to stand

2

the distant spire
pierces a retiring blue sky
bells scatter the air into notes
childhood faith shattered
the crud of doubt reframes the vision
elusive as the horizon

3

betrayal brands its mark
burns on flesh
illusion sears to truth
the wound in its rawness aches
and journey back to self
treads on emptiness

anzac

we leave our warm bed
rugged up from cold
before dawn
gather
with hundreds
out of the dark
around a cairn of unknown names

silence is broken only by coughs
and crunch of autumn under foot

no birds sing

the breeze sighs
trees weep
a solitary bugle plays

dark grief
for the futility of war
for humanity's inhumane bent

the soul of anzac
wings our nation's heart
hope rings in our song
as dawn pierces the inky sky

the first birds sing

escaping with cezanne

under his chestnut tree
bathers in naked strokes of light
pose
unburdened
i hear saplings crack in their play
and laughter as they lounge
in lusty rhythms of flesh
against blue
an illusion of reality

here free with the bathers
i am caught
in beauty
immersed
in their unfinished form
suspended from meaning

i am seduced
to linger
for the day
sheltered
under his chestnut trees

august mornings in hiroshima

1

a summer's day in august
with measured steps   i tread
once burnt ground

cicadas drum   humid air hums
distant streetcars rattle

weeping willows   green and dense
line the river's path
define this park of peace

i join those already at the cenotaph
the fragrance of incense and flowers
cannot ease the stark facts here

at the bronze sculpture
mother and child in firestorm
the mother's eyes stare with terror
as she hunches like an animal over her young

the tower clock strikes
its hands point to a moment that must not be lost
that mortal moment: eight-fifteen a.m.
my eyes catch hot hazy sky
old skin   innocence lost

2

that summer's day in august
the *enola gay* looms onto the horizon
a glint in the sun   a blinding flash
its shadow dooming humanity
its foreboding drone
drowned out by the song of cicadas

children chase dragonflies on their way to school
fishermen trawl the tranquil river
breakfast-cooking odours waft
the city bustles into life

supernatural light delivers hell to earth
hell is here
written on flesh without breath

3

a summer's day in august
stringed garlands of folded paper cranes
sway like multicoloured prayer flags
circling the children's peace monument

a mother kneels beside her young child
she tells a story
the story of sadako
sadako   who died of 'bomb sickness'
and inspired children
to fold paper cranes for peace

together the mother and child
step forward and ring the bell

above silhouetted against the sky
a sculpture of sadako   holds high a golden crane

hope balancing on its wings

at the nursing home

i fill the foot bath
my elbow checks the tepid water

she sits like a goddess at an altar
regal and stoic

her face shows many lifetimes
lipstick defines the line she desires
white wavy hair swept with combs
into a tight bun
gives the air of holding it all together

gently i hold and massage her feet
in the lavender scented water
feel a trembling and look up

tears run down her cheeks

she weeps the words
i haven't felt touch like this
for as long as I can remember

how to love a rock

its a hard thing to love a rock
you need to receive it as gift
spend time
commune
gaze
touch and stroke
its smoothness
and grooves
flaws and imperfections
hold and ponder
imbue the magic of its radiating warmth

wait upon it
allow it to seize your senses
listen for its whisper

consider where it belongs
maybe to spin joyfully back out to sea
maybe a memory of a beach walk
or friendship
to adorn your bookshelf or garden
or a bonsai pot
for a miniature fig to claim as its own

if it doesn't inspire
let it go

going going

the chainsaws stop

with night
possums scurry across the fence
over the ivy into the last blue gum

tiger eyes
in the dark   glow
white furry tails
curl flashes of light

they scramble
onto swaying melaleuca to feed
before they are off
for their night journey

on my morning walk
at the foot of a telegraph pole
a young ringtail possum lies
in sacrificial pose
electrocuted

in stiff smelling air
standing alone on the street
i look at the bare spaces in the sky
and rage
against the taking of our treescape

hiroshima sixty-five years on

sings a song of hope
cicadas have the upper note
the coo of doves
like tenors ground the sound
cooling water trickles
and children play

incense wafts from beds of sand
people bow as they pass
coloured cranes like prayer flags
hang on trees
and memorials

today is warm   balmy
i sit by the river near the epicentre
it is 8.15 a.m.

bells
ring out across the peace park
and around the city

fromelles 2009

time
exposes
bones
in *no man's land*

stories shout
from mass graves

hell-trap stories
gallant stories
fear-filled stories

failure crawls
through fire
mud   barbed wire
piteous writhing mates
drainage ditches
no respite

blinkers of youth
lure of adventure
crippled
nightmared

an emotional cry
will you not fight for land your fathers died for

and wars roll on
deafened with enterprise

now i ask how can cycles have an end

2009 – mass graves began to be exhumed, remains being identified
and laid to rest with honour: it brings to the fore once again a story
of the worst 24 hours in australian history, 19 july 1916, 5,533
australian casualties in one night and with no ground taken

chance encounter

my rustling disturbed his place
how long he watched
i do not know
but hopped off to a safer space

then stopped
turned
looked again

our eyes met
both stood still
two of us alone
in the bush

yearning to bridge the gap
i reached out my hand
a divide
like two pots of gold
without a rainbow
held us apart

for a moment
i breathed his fear
our eyes were held
alert…focused
a glint of knowing
crossed the stare

this proud grey
the hunted
knowing his place
turned
and bound away

dispossession

memories

black marble horsemen
with medals and guns
celebrating spanish conquests in chile
dominate santiago's *plaza de armas*

i linger by an abstract monument
catching morning light
history's cry is its caption
without our land there is no life

massive basalt boulders
circle like a gossip of standing stones
and mounted high
on a roughly hewn second tier
chiselled cracked and cut
as if lightening split the rocks
a shadowed noble face
bigger than life

its carved wistful eyes
look beyond the plaza people and pigeons
to the mountain
once home of the *mapuche* people

around the base children play
lovers cuddle   adults chatter
while first people still with indomitable spirit
bear memories of dispossession

dispossession 2

powerless

today a dusty sun slants sepia light
an eerie still scene of a shanty town
on the outskirts of lima in peru

monotone brown
ruins   rubble   rubbish   scant vegetation
brown   dusty brown

the dispossessed
in makeshift shelters
never ending palette of desolation

here on the outskirts of lima
like a barnacled mass they cling

one night ten years ago
in india
i lay in your arms weeping for the poor
having seen the sorrow in a mother's eyes
felt the touch of a begging hand
and i asked why

here they do not look
they turn away
a water truck comes
to refill drums
for those who can afford water
earlier it had freely watered green grass
of our resort with its luxury pool

when i walk away
i do not weep
answers would choke with dust
i don't even know the questions
just crave your arms around me
against this inequality

dispossession 3

out of sight

dry dusty shanty town
make-shift poverty
clammers on the fringe of our resort
south of lima in peru

the solid stone wall
divides us
out of sight
but not out of mind

tokyo markets

1

jammed with strolling locals
baskets and bags knocking and nodding
bustling shoulder to shoulder
the markets absorb
and huddle the people
here it is about the splurge of living
here life pulsates
under swaying red lanterns

a lively buzz and brackish tang
lures me
to a cool sea-wash briny world
octopus tuna and sword fish
on rock salt and ice
eyes stare blankly
lobsters tap   panic-like   the glass of the tank
mackerel beat their tails in a shallow dish
crabs crawl and clamour over each other
a gasping fish with throbbing gills
waits on a sacrificial wet greyscale altar
deep guttural cries and skilled hands
men in wet galoshes and plastic caps
tout their wares sharpening their knives

a willow of a boy in the corner
with *kokoro* and pride in his stance
chants a mantra to buy his shrimp
his shrill soprano voice
in harmony with the rhythm of the sea
catches me as water sloshes underfoot

2

vendors flaunt boxes of sweets
their chants like a rehearsed choir
blend in harmony
pasted deep red *azuki* beans
coloured in chestnut   hydrangea blue
cherry blossom   peach and grape
are jellied and displayed

the pied pipers of the food markets
in coloured caps cry out *oishi oishi*
and woo with samples on bamboo toothpicks
from sizzling pans and hot plates
crisp aromas waft
crowds swarm like bees to a hive
at displays of *tempura teriyaki sushi* and *soba*
each on a bed of fringed green plastic leaves

i am immersed in chaos of humanity
and feel at home

kokoro: with heart feeling energy
oishi: delicious
azuki beans: red-skinned sweet beans; basis of most japanese sweets

soka-eki

there is nothing poetic here
a language i cannot understand
faces i cannot read
ways i do not comprehend
only the cicadas i know
yet even their stinging ring
is alien to my ear

tokyo train

on a train
in cramped and swaying space
grey suited briefcase smells
stuffy conforming silence

speed shifts the strap i grip
feet rock in time to its rhythm
a dark blur of mean-shaped high-rise
corridor the tracks

blank faces caught
in alien worlds of electronics
outside flashing neon shout at numbness

we the night commuters
a brace of anonymity
breathe each others air
and pretend we're not there

only my eyes out the window
beam as i glimpse the moon smiling on me
as she does on you in a distant land

Cockatoo clamour

upon waking

a sulphur-crested morning
the backyard's old blue gum
delighted
in cockatoo clamour

its boisterous energy
devoured the dull silent air
lifted the oyster-grey sky
and like a wild orchestra

swept up the broken pieces
of my night into a new day

the black-shouldered hawk

with dawn
into my view
on the wing of the ocean breeze
up-wind riding
came an air-faring mariner
wingspan in full command
on the lightness of air
with tail fluting ripples of gold
a frisson of dawn-light
shimmering
it hovered like a sky-cheetah
in search of its prey
and held me

then away on air currents it soared
leaving me lead-footed
in wet sand

crimson rosella

sun's shock and shimmer
like a swift air brush
on its fluted tassel

winged pimpernel of the bush
zips past
te deum ringing for soulmates
engaged to ignite eros

sharp streak   into the day
flash of chilli-red cuts the air
tosses high on a stringy-bark

orion-fire
scarlet beauty in midnight blue
its ruffle
spins to a blur

aerodynamics of a feather

a spent feather lay
pinioned
by tiny beads of dew
which in my hand roll and fall
and here it is

sulphur-yellow runs
like a scale of music
along its white quill

thousands of sinewy notes
hairs   each fine as breath
velcroed into one
with nylon tenacity
to ride the toughest day

and now what use
except to put in my cap
and marvel
at aerodynamics

a black swan event

see on a lonely stretch of water
a wind choreographed dance
of black swans
noble stance
elegant moves
they dabble in brackish shallows
close in amongst the reeds

was it a shifty wind
that blew them in
was it the algae and duckweed
that lured them
rare on this side of the lake

they dip their red beaks
then their long curved necks
like question marks
lift   and stretch

sometimes not so elegantly
they up-end
bottoms in the air
black tutus flounced

some lift off fleetingly
with a wonk wonk wonk
running on water across the lake
wide white-tipped black wings
bellow-beat the water
and   with a whistling sound
like ballerinas glide back

how i'd like to get closer
even for a moment
let them know i am their friend
they are aware of me
and with each of my forward steps
they languidly glide further away

baptism by fire

after the rain
grass shines

air tingles
skin   like a lover's touch

a raindrop catches the sun
with a cheeky wink

rainbow lorikeets
swinging topsy-turvy

like sugar eating acrobats
dressed in clown suits

splay spindles of red bottle brush
on water-laden branches

when they see me
a boisterous hurly-burly
flutter of wings

flares like bright flames into the sky
and in their helter-skelter

a shower of a thousand raindrops
shocks me back to earth

learning to take time

i watch you   white-chested shag
steady on ash-grey rock
your wings preened to the sun
a black triangular shawl
hang-glider steady
like one who studies air currents
i watch you watch the morning
and learn to take time

wild no longer

in northern queensland
we drove up the dirt track
to the co-op
where they sell tools   seeds   sprays
and superphosphate

there i met the cockatoo

tis no one's pet   caught years ago
like a mascot it is
that old rusty cage been under the pepper tree now for eons
it gets a feed
it's only dusty 'cause it don't get the wind or rain
being close to the dirt road don't help
used to be out on a chain got too vicious
don't let a child close
or putcha finger in
it bites

a sharp mangy face stared at me
claws
clubbed now   arthritic
clung to the perch

it shifted balance
as i watched
its lifeless feathers on one wing fanned
exposing a shot of dull satin green

i remembered as a child releasing my father's prized birds
i only wanted to be their friend
let them play for awhile in the blue sky
i thought they would come back
she's only a child my mother said
she doesn't understand

now i'm not a child   i do understand
I couldn't free the cockatoo

www.ingramcontent.com/pod-product-compliance
Lightning Source LLC
Chambersburg PA
CBHW070919080526
44589CB00013B/1357